Everything is Water

EVERYTHING IS WATER

Poems by Greg Chaimov

PRESS-22
PORTLAND, OREGON

Acknowledgments

A version of "The Ohio 1950 Thanksgiving Record Snow" appeared in *The Oregonian* newspaper. Versions of "Under the Great Calabash Tree," "The Face," "Book Tour," "The Ascent of Man," and "A Poet Named Northern Island" appeared in the *Legal Studies Forum*; these poems, with versions of "Fever," "So Sweet a Lament, that the Winds Might Have Stopped to Listen," "Torch Song," "Conversation by the Neva," and "*Sacrum Commercium*," were included in *The Old World*, a limited-edition chapbook published by the William Stafford Center of Lewis and Clark College.

Copyright © 2010 by Greg Chaimov. Book design and production by John Laursen at Press-22. Cover photograph by Eric Brandt. All rights reserved. No part of this book may be reproduced or transmitted in any form or by any means, electronic or mechanical, including photocopying, recording, or by any information storage and retrieval system, without the permission in writing from the copyright owner.

ISBN 978-0-942382-13-6

Press-22

4828 Southeast Hawthorne Boulevard

Portland, Oregon 97215

To the memory of my grandparents, R. E. and Mary Dimick

Contents

At the Harrowing

Under the Great Calabash Tree *3*

Willing the World *4*

Now Is the Time *5*

Rebirth *6*

The Night Sky Is Never Bigger than on the Road Home *7*

A Lifetime *8*

Gall and Wormwood *10*

On the Going-to-the-Sun Highway *11*

Until They're Lost *12*

Grail Quest *13*

Boxed In *14*

A Distant Freight Train's Howl *18*

Past Tense *19*

Dancing Lessons

Dancing Lessons *25*

Fever *26*

Casus Belli *27*

So Sweet a Lament, that the Winds Might Have Stopped to Listen   28

The Face   29

Homecoming   30

Astrophil and Stella   32

Taxonomy   34

A History of the World   36

Off Shore   37

On Foreign Shores

Torch Song   45

Baptism   46

Book Tour   47

Cascade Starlight   48

The Ascent of Man   50

A Poet Named Northern Island   51

On the Rue   52

Orpheus and Eurydice   54

On Pierce Street   55

The Left-Handed Hummingbird   56

Conversation by the Neva 58

The Ohio 1950 Thanksgiving Record Snow 59

Philosophers' Stone

Progress 63

Sacrum Commercium 64

I Shall Be Telling This with a Sigh 65

Palimpsest 66

Narcissus 67

Lamentation 68

Life Imitating Art 70

Good Fences 72

Silences 74

On Humboldt Bay 76

December Mornings 77

Notes 81

Everything is water and the world is full of gods.
 —Thales of Miletus

At the Harrowing

Under the Great Calabash Tree

Like the antique clock my brother presented
one birthday that's blurred with all the rest:
You spin the tiny knob backwards to head
the hands in the path of time's advance. Best
to believe it's like the orchard cut back
to foster a better crop, or the freeze
the backyard cherries need before their black
and yellow fruit can drop. How else to conceive
of the loss of one so dear, to survive
in the silence that follows like hands
pressed against the ears? To begin a life
again after reason returns and grants
the chance to recover the years you'd tossed
into vidual winds or pinned upon a cross.

Willing the World

You track the lifts
and falls, skin slack
over ribs you swear
weren't there before,
each breath more shallow,
or so you hope:
willing such stillness
into the sunlit room
that even the motes
will stop floating
so that your guilt
will stop, as if your wishes
added to the world
any more than when
you were a little boy
refusing to wash your socks
so long as the team
you loved
kept on winning.

Now Is the Time

Now is the time to visit the old man
I will become: his hearing, like the years,
far gone. He can't tell whether the *creak*
is a jay or the birch rubbing against the plank fence
because the wind has mustered the strength
to crest the hill now that the trees
are nearly bare. He hopes the jay,
giving pay to one of those bastard squirrels
that's always digging holes in his lawn.
If it's wind, then rain is coming in
and he can look forward to another night
of his joints aching as if he had taken
the advice of that young fool of a doctor
who's forever after him to make use
of the gym pass the children have given him.
He hopes the jay. Jays are among the few things
that remind him of being a boy.
Laughter. Kites. The intermittent *thud*
of walnut husks. Everything else takes aim
at the part of him that feels as if
the world around him has vanished
or will vanish if he looks at it long enough.

Rebirth

In memory of Barrett Forst Ugland

Grief is a tree
easier borne
when bare; it's
new green shoots
that make us aware
of the pain
wombed through many
moonless weeks, the
kiss of sun-fledged
air waking us
from the dream
into which, as
soon as we saw
the worn leaves
loosed, we sought to sink
our deepest roots.

The Night Sky Is Never Bigger
Than on the Road Home

Even for Montana that first breath
of winter had come on soon. Three weeks
before Veterans' Day and you could feel
the stubble wheat break under your boots.

Ron and I had sipped Wild Turkey to fuel
our shouldering the mile plus of gravel road
from slaughterhouse to bed. A furlong in,
a wether lamb was champing on orchard grass.

Moon thrown from his wool guided us
over the stile. Whether youth made the lamb
brave or stupid didn't matter:
he wasn't skittish till we bent to slit him.

We told each other that coyotes would've
got him by Christmas, that he was like
Ron's baby brother Ed, who was sure
he'd never die right up until the balloon
burst, the heroin firing his gut
like the sun on Icharus's wings.

A Lifetime

Maybe the breeze carries a whiff
of Cavendish or the sunset flashes
a certain shade. He's beside you again,
your father, sharing this scratch of wool.

You inhale the sky, the constellations
he recites, the shapes of clouds that come
to cover. Forty years have passed, a lifetime
in some lands. Every evening at this hour,

a gust from the sea streams through the gap
in the hills, the air cools and the fir boughs pitch
with a hiss more remembered than heard.
Beneath the firs: tiny birds — sparrows,

you presume; overhead, swallows leave the eaves.
The walnut trees are down, split and stacked
against the north wall. The deodar cedar
you planted as a child sheds thick needles,

which, when you forget to rake, will suffocate
the lawn the way your father died, bereft
of even his name. But tonight, he's telling
again of the ancient inland sea —

dry-grass hills specked with sage, hills he hiked
in search of lives no one had found before:
whelk, whorl, Mesozoic krill. He's telling,
too, about dust's coloring the dusk,

his cutting scrub for the fire, his stumbling
upon the brass-yellow vein that made his heart
beat like a squirrel's. He'd counted the stars
to stay awake, hearing boots in every rustle.

Then, dawn disclosed his mistake: "Pyrite,"
he laughs, tongues tobacco from a tooth.
"That one night," he says, and shakes his head,
"I felt I'd won – for once, I'd proved them wrong."

Without looking down, he gives your thigh
a squeeze. "At least, I'd known the feeling."
There's no more talk, just the even breaths
of your pup asleep on the last patch of lawn

still warm from the summer sun. And you wish now,
as you'd wished then, to know what your father
had felt, and more than that, you wish
you could have been to him that golden rock.

Gall and Wormwood

On that early morning, fog floated
over the water like the Spirit's hovering
in that time before time began. A bird — sleek, black,
long-necked — slapped at the waves with its wings.
On the path beside the bank, two lovers
trapped inside solitude saw in that flight
the final fragment of their dying universe.
They could not recall the past with delight
or anything approaching nostalgia.
Their savage mockery of God — rutting
into madness in a corner of the convent —
had brought revenge: the cutting
that left the both of them bereft. His wound
had healed; hers, they understood, never would.

On the Going-to-the-Sun Highway

The sweep of the road echoes the sweep
of the mountain peaks. If you look hard,

the guidebook says, you can see the nimble
mountain goats pick their way up craggy slopes.

They're searching for salt. The book natters on
about the lives of the herders who brought

the first Merinos from their faraway
corner of Spain. At the edge of a grove,

mistaken by most for a boulder,
slumps an earthen hut that's survived

nearly a hundred winters — eighty more
than the couple whose bleached crosses

you notice when you turn back to your car,
crosses wreathed in neoprene flowers —

the only brilliance in miles of pine
and slate, beseeching us to believe

that the garishness of man is
what's needed in God's garden to be seen.

Until They're Lost

The slap of tiny slippers on cold tile.
Buds from bulbs long forgotten.
Smile of one too young for guile.
Hand upon your neck when least expected.
Comma to your sleeping parentheses.
Skein of thought, like a hummingbird,
                caught before its flight.
A meal cooked just for you.
Red roads. Dog's snore. December light.
Waking as for the first time to even breaths.
The quiet that falls with snow.
A head on your chest, no matter whose.
That, once in a while, life is easier
                when you've grown old.

Grail Quest

In memory of Tom Sandberg

We thought you fought going into that good night,
so restless were you, as if the next day
a Bulgar you might meet on a search for gas
would invite us into his home to stay,
or once more you'd bundle us for sleep
on a monastery's cold stone floor.
We imagined there still must be places
in the world you wanted to take us,
although none of us could guess a campground
we might have missed. No boys could have learned
more of the world than we, walking the walls
that god-like Odysseus breached with his horse,
reliving that last full measure of Maine
Volunteers. No boys could have learned more
about how to be a parent or friend:
to be present in a loved one's life,
no matter how many miles you had to drive,
or at what time. We thought you fought
going into that good night until we pieced
together that you knew you were headed
into the one land you'd never seen,
into the one land where you'd find the peace
you always wished for us. And for this world.

Boxed In

If I'd raised myself from the chair and stood,
I could've reached the switch. Instead, I let
the twilight lengthen, let it linger
and darken the room. After forty-five years,
the old man had dropped his mask, and I
was afraid to look. We faced each other —
silhouettes all anyone would've seen.
One sound only punctuated our breaths:
the *clink* of ice on glass. He thought I'd wanted
to interrogate him, to hear him admit
that, to me, he was just a son of a bitch.
That's why the catch, the slight jerk of the head,
when I started to talk about me, not him.
He'd expected the bourbon to free
my anger, had taken his as a vaccine.
The softness in my voice must've surprised him,
let me in where he hadn't intended.

That morning, I'd attended the sale
of an old woman's things. The company hired
to dispose of the lot had posted rules,
taped them high on the door: *No dickering
before noon (we haven't had our coffee).
We reserve the right to refuse. . . .*
Tables displayed the usual junk: self-help

books, plastic globe labeled Nantucket,
casino tumblers, plates the children
hadn't wanted. A large, felt-skinned cube,
its latch a sideways shepherd's crook. "Hat box,"
the seller offered when I looked confused.
Under the lid, trimmed slip of yellowed newsprint:
Death Claims Child Dancer. Seven when she died,
the story said, a burst appendix.
Photographs, faded grays, pasted to thick
cardboard cards, like the kind that backed
stereopticon views: at the barre,
a younger Dame Margot Fonteyn in arabesque
and attitude. Consummate artist,
this young girl: not once a smile or even
a glance at the mustachioed man
I imagined barking commands from behind
the camera. Clipped reviews. Pink ballet shoes.
Dried wrist corsage: gardenias tied with satin.
Handkerchief wrapping violets. A program
or two from recitals for royalty
waiting out revolts in Europe. Funeral
notice: Strauss's *Cinderella* — her favorite —
piped on the organ. Governor's condolences
read by a bishop. Mile-long cortege. Sorrow
from as far as Veracruz. Not one item

to tell a person whether she was kind
and generous. What she craved and feared.
Whether she danced to please herself or others.
When I held up the box, the cashier barked
twenty-five dollars — a price I considered
high even for a life so poignant.

My father, drunk and deep in the wing-back
chair, must've thought I'd come for confession,
his reasons for leaving so often, for treating
my mother as an undisciplined daughter.
Out it all came between yawns, swigs
of Ancient Age: the anger, the belief
that she'd betrayed, not he. It took some minutes
of his shaking his head for him to understand
that I wasn't after the demons
that had tormented him. I wanted to hear
the things he'd have put in my box. I'd brought
my own list to compare: Brownie shot
of the buzz-cut boy clutching the brand-new
football he was supposed to enjoy.
The butterfly collection, desiccated
beside its first-place ribbon. The steel sprinkler
that splashed him until his father, more fueled
than the mower, ran the thing over. Grades —

perforated from the tacks his mother used
to stick them to the kitchen wall. I'd thought
my father would prick my pride, pick the wooden
racing car he'd finished when, to his eyes,
I'd botched the job. Then, about the time
the bottle drained, a grin closed the rest
of his face. He'd found a better way
to dose out pain: he had no idea,
he said, what he'd put into my box.

A Distant Freight Train's Howl

A lifetime beside her allows me
to know she's starting like she did
to murmurs from the crib. Vague Danish vowels
lilt again despite fifty years
on the Kansas plains. I kid her
about ears too keen for our modern times,
and at her sigh, I guide her to my pillow.
As she nestles in, it comes to me
she's in '58, meeting the gunner's mate
she wed, which explains the gasp,
the arching back as I press my lips
against her neck. I wish she moved for the grey
I've earned, but I've learned not to refuse
these last small measures of my youth.

Past Tense

I jotted *tesserae* on the blank page.
I'd heard the word used for a chestnut's leaves,
liked the quick three beats, hoped the term described
the jagged ridge across the lake. The next
sight to write was the carved stone spire, construction
I'd thought a rich man's vision of Arthurian
style. The spire rises a good hundred feet
from the lake's far shore. There's nothing more:
no bailey, no keep or palisade.
According to postcards, the building's called
the Kingfisher Tower, hewn from stone
in the second term of Ulysses Grant.
Oddly, locals don't know who built the tower,
its purpose, then or now. Once, a woman heard,
they'd held weddings on the grounds; another's sure
the structure started out a mansion
for a New York banker's lover. What I
want to know is how a fractional castle
can pass from memory after less
than a century and a quarter.
Some events we want to forget,
like that gin-drenched night on Union Bay
when predator became the prey.
It's the collective failure that puzzles.
Losing Stonehenge one can blame on Roman troops,

and the *moai* on Easter Island's seesaw
wars. These Leatherstockings have no excuse
for local amnesia. The town's heard not
an angry shot since the Treaty of Ghent.

In an old B & B, I finally find
a graybeard who tells: the tower lacked purpose
except to be built. From the beginning,
it's been empty, unused — a project to keep
masons employed. Their patron, a magnate
named Clark, modeled his spire on Medieval
palaces seen by the Rhine, an American
Hohenstaufen *Schloss*. (No different in kind,
I admit, than my choosing *tesserae*,
or Latin dice, mosaic bits, for jags
of misted ridge.) In clippings preserved
in the town's atheneum, Clark praises
his tower for forming "an objective
point in the scene" that Nature had composed
of water and trees — as if the happenstance
of green on beveled green couldn't inspire.

Give Clark his due: he chose his anachronism.
The rest of us live the past without
our knowing. Think of the times we've said
of a friend: "There she goes again." Each marriage

like the one before: another needy man
who'll buy her every want until that doting
isn't thrill enough. Remember how we swore
we'd heed Santayana, wouldn't repeat
our parents' mistakes, how we wouldn't make
our kids play sports they didn't enjoy?
What did we know then of inheritance?
Look at us now and see the same green eyes,
same too-thick brows, the brittle knees,
the backhand slap that loosens teeth.

Dancing Lessons

Dancing Lessons

His eyes glide from her face to the window,
intent on signs of the coming storm.
She takes that pebble's weight of silence
for a slight; beneath a surreptitious breath,
she damns his failing to praise the hair
braided to promenade in public view.
She never thinks the absence of truth
could be a gift, just as she never imagines
he knew she placed that hushed and hurried call
on her way to the fruit-monger's stall.

Back in the second-floor flat, she buffs the pear
on the denim she wears tight against her thigh,
offers the flesh of that fruit as she offers
her own: as if the taste is one
of many to come. She never thinks he knows
his bite will consign them to a life
they'll measure by the times they pass in step,
no more masters of the floating floor
than the linden leaves that spin in the wind
that leads rain clouds from the sea.

Fever

Put into words the hollow ache
that precedes the tears you have to stop
before they reveal how much she takes
of the very essence of the air, hot
from your lips to hers, as if she were
some form of succubus, drawing life
from the passion she inspires, yours for her,
you with hope of nothing in return, wife
or no wife making no difference
to a heart's pumping its chambers dry
to fill the void that grows with her silence,
her sighs, and those ambivalent eyes
that make you believe this ache at your pit
is the feeling for which you were meant to live.

Casus Belli

She'd tell her parents she's writing the story
of the Trojan War from Helen's point of view,
but their missing the irony would be
more painful than this age she's living through.
After they'd recovered from their surprise,
they'd launch into another quarrel:
Her father would start to patronize,
insisting she learn to read Homer
in the ancient Greek. When he'd returned
from his study bearing his college texts,
her mother would lash him for the illusions
he empowers. He'd counter that they're blessed
to have a woman in the house who knows
the Spartan queen from a line of clothes.

Off they'd go, disputing who's the martyr,
which the slave. Each calling the other
a name blacker than the first, until
the reason for the fight matters not at all.
So she keeps to herself that being free
tastes of the breeze on the wine-dark sea.

So Sweet a Lament,
That the Winds Might Have Stopped to Listen

Pork Chops: So Versatile — So Confusing.
The headline greets him across the table.
His heart, by turns, laughs and cries. He's reading
Ariosto again. The long battle
at the gates of Paris has just ended.
Between Montmartre and Montlhéry,
two young Saracen soldiers search the dead
for their fallen liege, their plan to bury
him as God commands. In a few short lines,
they, too, will die — cut down by a Christian
patrol. He'd like her to hear why he finds
this passage so moving, why the young sons
of a fictional Moor matter so much,
but he can't bring himself to interrupt.

The Face

You see, God blessed me with a memory
for faces. I'm spared those awkward moments
over plates of sourdough and brie
when she reminds you of the time you'd met
two months before, which is why I'm mystified
by my inability to place the face
across the row of seats. The deep brown eyes,
the cheeks that make her look as if escaped
from some painting by Vermeer. And those bangs. . . .
This is not a face a man should forget.
I can picture her standing on a stage
like the clever poet from Massachusetts
I should be enjoying, but can't because
I'm stuck on who to me this angel was.

Homecoming

You glare at me, contempt barely masked,
and ask, *What did you do while I was away?*
I'll give you credit for consistency:
Best defense is a good offense, you'd say.

It's not your turn to question; that right's mine.
I know why you left; I just don't see
why you took so long to come back home,
why you couldn't at least have phoned.

No, I don't want to hear about the hearts
and heads you've broken, the chances you took.
So you've brought lots of gifts — big whooping deal.
Gifts don't make up for a lost twenty years.

Guys crawl this place with wads to blow on me —
they're not pulling out just because you're here.
The law presumes you're dead. I could've had
any one of a hundred handsome men.

But I'd weave clothes for your old man, poor soul —
he's stooped from grief, his mind undone —
then I'd pull the threads, dream up an excuse
why I couldn't go out with anyone.

That's your problem, you see: you can't say no.
If a party needs a life, you've got to go.

I didn't matter enough — that's what hurts.
Blow your smoke up another girl's skirt.

I raised your only son into a man.
What of him? Or the old woman who
anointed your tired feet? The hired hand?
As you are, only the dog could know you.

Astrophil and Stella

1

Not at first sight, nor with a dribbled shot....

Surprised, but not shocked, by your open displays
of affection toward a not inelegant
older man. You needed to play
the sun to everyone else's planet.
I couldn't fault your desire. You were no
different from the other young courtesans
who dreamed one day you'd ascend the throne.
We talked once then, a conversation neither
could recall without the other's prompting:
your wanting knowledge that I didn't have.
A half decade later, when we're working
together, I'll say I'm drawn to your laugh
more than the beauty that turns others' heads.
You'll drop your eyes and smile at what I've said.

2

Stella, the only planet of my life. . . .

Your name evokes Brando's drunken bellow
into the dark New Orleans sky. Fury.
Rejection. Betrayal. Feelings I know
now thanks to you. A different legacy
could've been yours if you'd had the decency
to tell me when you knew your heart had turned.
You call yourself "the up-frontest of the
up-front gals." Maybe, I'll concede, you were
lying to yourself — not only to me.
I should shoulder a share of the blame — beguiled
by the brightest ball in the galaxy,
I saw in you the star the Magi followed
and not the quasar, black hole deep inside,
pulling in all light, including mine.

Taxonomy

"Larkspur. That one I know," Steve said. He bent at the waist, hands on his
    knees as if talking
to a child. They had started the climb early, and the sun, through the
    dawn's haze, appeared as the moon,
split by oaks that grew tangled, leafless, shattered by snow. He stepped aside
    when Anne's shadow
covered the pale blossoms at his feet. She paused for a meadowlark hidden
    in scrub to complete
its five-beat song, then pronounced "*Delphinium nuttallianum*." A nod his
    only response. He had come
to expect her needing his acquiescence, this aura of control. Once they had
    debated the variety
of Prairie Star: *Glabra*? *Parviflora*? Now, he caught her looking at him as
    she would a plant too ordinary
to record. Thoughts of Anne as she had been flitted through Steve's mind.
    In those days,
she searched for living matter, not entries on a ledger. He wondered if she
    classed him, and if so,
the name she gave. Up she led, path cut by the hooves of blacktail deer, by
    the horses and cattle
that, in summer, clustered near springs and the meadow grass the water
    fed. On the way to the crest,
they passed filaree, shooting star, broadleaf lupine, glacier lily; each plant
    she claimed by scientific name.
Past where desert parsley bloomed, beside haystack rocks, across a draw,
    hillsides grew in shades from olive

to aquamarine. At a stalk of pearl-white bells, she stopped and shook her head. He watched her flip
the pages, and before she could find the family or even the common name, he said "Death camas."

A History of the World

You'd never know to look at her that she's writing
a history of the world in her head —
a romance, paradise lost, beginning
with the Fall. Not to be regained, she's said,
until. . . . Well, that she hasn't figured yet.
Her Eden was a stucco house in town,
gentle spouse, and infant son. A compliment
(Damn him!) and double Scotch her fruited bough.
Offers of redemption are too numerous
to count, each man's price too dear. She'd prefer
a man who'd die for her — some noble purpose,
not her skirt. That's unlikely to occur:
her heart's like Lucifer's: *obdur'd* — just trouble
for those who would abuse freedom of the will.

Off Shore

1

"This is nuts." She's dug two scoops, Sumatra
roast, then stopped. One thought leaves the jumble
that's her mind: *Brew your own for a change.*
The dog's boarded; her brother's got the kids.

The weekend's theirs. And Richard? Richard's
sleeping off Drambui rocks. From the deck,
she can barely see the row of houses
on the street a half-lot closer to the beach —

upper floors that rise through fog that drifts in
from the shore to manzanita planted years
before as break against the southern breeze.
In her line of vision: chimney caps — sheet

metal formed to helmets of conquistadors.
In her breath, stove smoke filled with pine.
Beyond the mist, beyond the sight of land,
trawlers low like scattered Guernseys, mired.

2

At least Laplace didn't live to learn
that Heisenberg's proof put an end
to science's dream of a unified theory,
a predictable world, measures for each
of Heaven's things. The paradigm's a paradox:
the more light you beam, the less you can find
of a particle's place in time and space.

So, too, with lovers, Marcel discovers,
when he tries to regard Albertine's heart.
Passion's incandescence burns all objects
in its way; love, in its turn, decays.
Or perhaps it's as Henri Cole decrees:
love, disclosed, repels what it sees.

3

Her fury follows down the path, past
a rivulet, past wrack, past sentinel birds
on alders shorn of leaves; between houses,

hydrangeas' late fall clusters now a brittle
beige and cream. She meanders the storm-throw line,
studies carcasses (infant crabs, shells cleaned

by gulls), planed boomerangs of wood, kelp, scum
dried like marzipan, twisted nylon twine.
She's searching, but won't know for what or why
unless she lucks upon translucent rock.
It's agates she's after. Chalcedony. Grand
memory: when she was ten, she could spy

one every few yards, and by morning's end,
her hem overflowed. She'd supposed the sea
would replenish the stones, grind them smooth

until waves floated small ones to the foot
of the dunes. She wants that youthful faith restored,
distilled. These days, the beach is barren;

others' hands have gleaned the sands. Agates, mined
along the Parana in Uruguay
or Brazil, sold by size in boardwalk stores.

4

She wants to know what to do when the best part
of you goes missing. The agates in you.
She sometimes spots a Jesus sky, thinks the search
has ended in another's smile. Then she reads
she should be hunting in, not outside, herself.

That's where fear comes in. There's one loss worse
than transcendence that's disappeared:
losing hope you'll achieve the peerless again,
as when you probe your soul and know
you're as barren as the sand on which you walk.

5

Over the couch: tangles of Richard's auburn
hair. The speakers whisper *Gimmie Shelter*,
the song a buzz, not words. On the television,
men stroll a spread of green. He's started

the furnace, not built a fire. The picture
windows, wet as bathroom glass, have trapped
cannabis, coffee, sourdough toast. He pats
the cushion next to him, lifts a mug, and sips.

She laments that which separates men from apes.
This welling — this sting — would be easier
to understand if she could decide whether
to envy or despise his need for nothing.

ON FOREIGN SHORES

Torch Song

I'm reading *The Bird Frau* as starlings,
lured by the summer's last plums,
cyclone down to the concrete walk
to spatter like fat on the grill
of the southern bistro next door
from which the cook's music — all salt pork
and sassafras — colors the street,
brushes on cymbals that mimic the voice
of a woman, words too distant to be discrete.
I savor the serendipity
until I remember why I'm here
in this cumulus twilight in late July:
I'm looking for a girl who's hunting up
a forty-dollar acetylene rush,
and I'm listening more than looking
because I'll know her only by her song.

Baptism

An unbroken plain spans from Gdańsk
to Carpathian range: palimpsest
worn translucent less from stamp of hoof and boot
than one tongue's scourging another and another
until there abides only a silence
like the world she inhabits where no word
exists for her to describe the tautness
of the eyes in that resurgence of senses
that comes from cleansing in the same
brackish water into which she was born.

Ankles seized by briny mire — a sign
for the frustration she feels for not knowing
the English word for the swift breath
on being entered for the first time,
as she's being entered now by the sea
lapping cold against her thighs, swollen
with tide, soon to bathe her salt in salt,
allowing her to taste the language
in which she'd lived, even if the ancient music
no longer flows to her unbidden.

Book Tour

The jacket's photograph stares back,
but it's the title that arrests: *Cobalt
Miles of Sky*. When you recite the line
to your mind's ear, you know it's cummings
that you hear. A quick search confirms:
He'd been writing about a Paris scene —
a scene you remember from your time together,
she and you — and you wonder,
wonder at night and when days are like night
whether she picked the line
because of a memory of you,
or at least thought a little of you,
for it's been years since you've more
than seen her striding across the campus green
in a skirt too short for a woman her age,
which is, you know, exactly why she wears it.

Cascade Starlight

1

A hundred conversations made babel
by echoes off the station's marble walls,
a hubbub that might as well be silence
or a foreign tongue: High German, perhaps,
the diesel taking me back to Cologne
and the cathedral's spires shadowing
like condor wings the bright Medieval square,
the same late-setting sky that prints the trestle
we're crossing onto boat-infested swells.

2

There's a spark in the tone of the woman
three seats ahead. I can't hold her words
any more than I can the birds that flee from the trees
along the tracks when the horn blares
the hobos away. Like careless left-hand fingers,
the rumble of wheels, steel on steel,
as if racing to catch the melody. This is how
a person hears Bach's *D Minor Toccata and Fugue*
in the far reaches of the cathedral:
not as jumble, but as sadness deep beneath the song.

The Ascent of Man

A thick-ankled girl of nineteen conveyed
by underground train. The kerchief she wrings
flames green in the bright strobing light. She's made
the decision to beg forgiveness, confessing
her sins to the wife whose spouse broke his vows
in her bed. Why? We won't know. A modern
poet tells no stories. For Pound,
the crowd of Metro platform passengers
suggested *petals on a wet, black bough*. Pleasing,
but no more. We learn nothing of morals,
of heroes, the cost of Achilles's craving
Bresies. It's a blame we must share: we'll
all choose kaleidoscope views to an errand
whose sense only the ancients commanded.

A Poet Named Northern Island

"The world's most famous dissident poet"
sits on a riser, eating a cookie.
The timid few who enter late will sit
far from the stage as if this were Shunyi
and his dissidence were a contagion.

Later, he will rail against the epithet,
blaming American propaganda:
A poet is a poet, he protests,
then offers lines that feature tea, the sea
his father's death, a city where *bird roads
define the sky*.
                The price of honesty:
His life in the language in which he wrote.
The most difficult lesson in this new
land? His learning to live in solitude.

On the Rue

The *Magnolia Soulengeana* shades the fenced café, sheds pink and scentless
    petals onto cast iron tables —
decorates as if the *maitre d'* had planned the tree's display to celebrate a
    saint's day or delivery of a beaujolais.
Blooms descend. The head waiter tends a woman whom his men address as
    the *Comtesse*, her French a task:
vowels stretched by American Midwest. Each time the men slip their money
    from the mat, the Comtesse peels
the roll in her lap; the replenished stack curls like the magnolia flowers that
    wait to land. The boy who clears
her plate compares a blossom to her saucer — with free hand cupped, he
    explains the tree in children's pidgin:
"*Deux cents ans — de Japon.*" From the woman the youth receives five *franc*
    note and grateful nod. Taxis' engines
echo off macadam; exhaust that blows from under buses scatters sparrows
    that compete for specks caught
between the ancient cobbles. When the *Comtesse* has finished her sixth or
    seventh absinthe, an old man,
Algerian by birth, steps from the magnolia's trunk. As he has each
    afternoon that week, he tucks a dachshund
into the miniature bed he's built from a grocer's crate, pushes the cart until
    the frame nudges
the *Comtesse*'s waiting leg. "*Par hasard,*" the *Comtesse* starts, as if the old
    Algerian has appeared
at her side for the very first time. "*Je cherche . . .*" she resumes. The man's
    somber shake, the words

that follow, like the buses' fumes to the flock of birds, whisk her voice away.
> No matter how many bills

she thrusts at the shopworn fingers, the beret he clutches, "*Je suis navre*" is
> all that he will say.

Her eyes narrow, wet from the bronze of the fading sun in the windows
> across the square. She gazes

past the man to the passengers who flow from the Metro doors like the
> petals from the magnolia,

and says to anyone close enough to hear: "I thought for sure he'd come
> today."

Orpheus and Eurydice

In the tedious hour after sex,
the couple will quarrel over whether
their turbaned cabbie came from Eritrea
or some other East African land. For now,
they're relieved to have at the wheel
a man the shade of the souls who haunt
the darkened streets he ferries them on.

Each day in Mogadishu, the driver studied
the white officers in wraparound glasses
who paid what he asked for his melons.
That's how he learned to read a fare
without meeting eyes in the rearview mirror.
That's how he knows the man's grip relaxes
when the taxi spans the bridge across
the city's DMZ, how he knows
the couple's passion won't survive
when he hears her bark "Don't look at me."

On Pierce Street

The castle theme repeats from room to room,
begins at the armored suit that's posted
in the hall to welcome guests, continues
through smoky etchings they've hung at the head
of the stairs and the tapestries tacked over
walls. As in Victorian homes, the light's
dim, even at midday, windows colored
to match cathedral glass. Some days, you might
think yourself in Lincolnshire or Kent. Ask
for the tour of antique goblets, their own
holy grails, to hear the tales they love best.
They take their refuge in this keep and don't know
that, as in mist-wrapped Camelot, there's danger
in playing at Guinevere and Arthur.

The Left-Handed Hummingbird

The Aztecs never employed the wheel
except for the small movements of toys, yet
they spread Tenochtitlán, Mexican Venice,
across a lake's meshed canals, fed themselves
from floating gardens, erected temples
to rival the pharaohs'. Cortés's soldiers
"gawped like hayseeds at the wide streets," the carved
stone beasts, the markets bright with bounty
from hundreds of miles: jade, gold, copper, feathers.
None of this saved the natives from carnage.
The Aztecs' codex of conquests ends
with cannon, harquebus and steel,
the Empire of the Sun ground beneath
Spaniards' wheels. Perhaps the king,
his philosopher-priests, should've made more
of the wheel; then again, you can't know
what you don't until the consequences
occur. Take me, a man gifted at love.
Not conqueror. A man who listens and learns
another's dreams, favorite Braque,
that she takes her tea with room for cream,
that her birthday's the same as Yo-Yo Ma's.
You couldn't count the times she's opened a box
wrapped in chiffon to match the flowers, found
a gift she'd never suggested, that I'd seen

reflected in her eyes. Surely, that care
should be courting enough to enjoy
the passions due a perpetual groom.
That's, she complained, my flaw: I can't feel
her thrill at a painting's blocks of beige
and brown, or how a Celtic hymn brings her
to tears. And the worst of it is, she said,
I don't even know the connection's missing,
can't understand her choosing a man
who's more than a mirror. That every flower
offered was a narcissus. As if
that's my undiscovered wheel, why I'm left
to sit at this desk flipping through drawings,
the legends, of ancient Indians.

Conversation by the Neva

"Only the midwife, God, and you," confesses
the dancer to the Russian duke — the father
who learns, to his surprise, that he misses
the stillborn boy, this son of whom he'd heard
not a word in the thirty Julys
since that night outside the Tuileries
when duke and dancer raveled knitted lives.
He can't be sure whether to believe — she's
still the same coquette she always seemed;
her story could be bait for ancient sturgeon.
After supper, hounds dreaming at his feet,
he'll ponder his wanting the little one
he couldn't have known — and not the old love
who recalls for him the youth that he was.

The Ohio 1950 Thanksgiving Record Snow

A mark of winter is time to remember
life's early loves — memories as mantled
as the sedans that were banked *for white miles*
on the side of the road to the farmhouse
to which you'd escaped after the Grange-hall dance,
where, from your second-floor room, roofs resembled
humped cows snuffling for grass
beneath the twenty-two inches of snow
that had fallen since you'd left off spinning
all by yourself under the blue lights
by the stage, just beyond the trumpet's shaded
arc of sound, the room from where you saw
Chesterfields lightning-bug behind windshields
lacquered with breaths you'd heated — turned quick
and thick with a single flip of your hair —
while headlights searched the gaps
between trunks of trees and looked as surprised
as the drivers had been by the storm
off the lake the radio hadn't predicted.

Philosophers' Stone

Progress

It's 6 a.m. in midwinter. The moon,
a sliver from full, ghosts the ridge of trees.
The dawn begins to spark on homes across
the stream. My dogs have yet to see the geese

asleep in drifts of leaves. The only sounds
besides their *huffs* are water's rilling sand
and the drone of distant engines. An hour,
and then the men will descend, tools in hand,

to frame the house that's rising from the bank
to block the views of neighbors up the slope.
In this result, I find the metaphor
my mind's been seeking since I woke.

Sacrum Commercium

The legacy of human exchange:
In a barren sea, alien isopods,
sluiced with ballast from passing ships, invade
the estuaries, floating until caught
in the gills of the mud-dwelling shrimp
who will serve as their hosts. The order
of devastation will be evident
only when bass and merganser
litter the sands we like to walk.
Then, we'll remember how the cycle starts,
how failure comes to gnaw deep in the gut:
it burrows in when we open our hearts
in a chance exchange, a smile that leaves us flushed
and aching for a chance to touch.

I Shall Be Telling This with a Sigh

It's like when you drive with the windows fogged:
You know the danger, but press on.
This blindness you believe to be a blessing.
If you could see, you'd only take the road
toward disappointment once again.
Recall the boy who pedaled dark streets
beneath bats that careened after moths
that hovered by lights — lights that shone
under crowns of maples that hid the beams
that swept the sky — the boy who imagined himself
in *War of the Worlds*, the searchlights seeking
Martian ships, the boy who hoped a carnival
waited, offering rides ten for the dollar.
The boy who'd go, although he knew he'd find
no more than a furniture store or new
line of Ford, it being enough that his presence
caused the streetlights to cycle on and off.

Palimpsest

A field of grass aflame
in autumn shades.
The sea is not the sea
and I am not myself.
And so it begins:
The pull of tides,
the pulse of blood. . . .
The roar in my ears
that would be wind
or winter's waves in flood.

The gulls are singing benisons
to the last light of the sun,
while my soul drifts, unmoored,
face lit from below,
waiting out of my reach
for the flash of green
that means
        money or love
or nothing at all.

Narcissus

After Robes of the Gods*, by Theodore Weiss*

As a wave shouldered in by typhoon winds topples when the trough jolts
        the ocean floor like a boy
who dashes down a slope, unaware of the root on which he'll stumble, only
        soft, soft hands to cushion
his fall, *so the gods use us*. So we allow each other to believe, the gods being
        our creation to relieve
the shame of having forged this darkness we bequeath. Take that boy who,
        when a man of abundant years,
confronts his mirror, hunting the bloom once accepted as his due. His
        mind would refuse, leaving pain akin
to a phantom limb's were it not for his heart that forever remembers the
        yellow chiffon, that not-so-stolen kiss,
blossoms from late Rome apples dropping onto the pond. Boats folded from
        librettos plucked from
trampled August grass: Bizet and Debussy bobbing in ripples. The night
        breeze that fires the paper lanterns
dangling from wires: a flare, then ash, black through black — the way the
        stream passed beneath the bridge
where his boats began to float from sight, granting him wishes not to come
        true until, like Penelope,
he stopped willing the horizon to yield a mast and bent to the life the gods
        had deigned to grant.

Lamentation

1

Study Stieglitz's masterpiece and you'll find
a scene that seems mere happenstance
becomes composed as any master's canvas.
Follow the gangplank's line, the looping rails.
Track the deepening shadows, those spots of white:
anxious face, brimmed hat caught by sun.
Diagonals lead the eyes in, in past
the balance of bright and black. It's not
that he's captured the passengers posing
or gotten lucky with his lens: he sees
the order in chaos better than other men.

2

Some law of optics must account for why
a snapshot's background seems so much farther
than the same scene does to the naked eye.
Half-built high-rise. Scaffolding and crane.
They towered that late Bangkok afternoon;
now, you view a woman washing clothes
against a rock, an old man, bathing,
covered with tattoos. Beside them floats
the carcass of a dog, black and white garnish
on a river that flows the shade and texture
of Thanksgiving gravy. Closer still,
two shadows, one longer than the other,
stretch from the ferry's rail. Of this scene,
there's everything you'd want to know except
why those shadows haven't merged as one.

Life Imitating Art

The landscape's misted in the sketch, and her
eyes, that pale ocean green, seem live
as if lit from behind, sun through leaves.
The painter decides which of many sheets
of penciled poses will grant that someone
lifetimes beyond the time no life remains.

Passion's perfection through obsession remains
the artist's technique for capturing her
spirit, turning an emblem into someone
seen from within and without. To keep alive
that kind of religion requires the scrawled sheets
to carry meanings beyond their scenes: leaves

as hard death and resurrection, not leaves.
Danger comes when the artist observes the remains
of their interrupted meal, and his sheets,
wet, lie in a tangle that mimics her
hair. He's crossed his Rubicon and must live
with her having become more than someone.

There should be a tug of regret. Someone,
anyone, else would see the risk he leaves
for himself. You might ask: How can he live
the scene he's painting? How much remains
that's not part of him? Not of the two? Her
ocean-green eyes reflect his, the sheets

around her soaked in his scent. Apples. Sheets.
The sea. Fragrance of linseed. Things someone
else might perceive objectively, but her
lasting presence in this, his existence, leaves
him struggling to render what remains
of his world, to find his lost craft, to live

with axis restored, as a monk can live
on work and prayer. He can't discard the charcoaled sheets
or erase until no trace remains.
Another solution: turn to someone
who'll stay discrete. She does as he asks and leaves.
The fool, he believes he'll choose the memories of her.

You see, we'll think we can live without that someone,
then salt remains on the sheets when she leaves
and in that thin indentation of her.

Good Fences

According to the town's gazette, the afternoon snow would fall for an hour
      or less. That prospect of white
must've kept my eyes on the low slate sky, kept me from noting straight
      away the bare bedraggled mound
beside the path. By nightfall, I learned a county crew had torn down the
      barn where my neighbor stored
his '47 Farmall A, blades the tractor pulled, hoe and spade with handles
      bleached as any beach's drift.
In their place, rodents' holes the coyotes had exposed; volunteer barley
      burred ground not seen
before that day, though I'd walked the fence in all weathers. Between split
      timbers, dimpled glass
had hung, panes scored like cataracts, pocked with holes from errant shots.
      The one thing I thought
I'd miss: the metal roof alive with *pings* in ricocheting summer rain. Past
      where the barn had stood:
Apple trees. Bare. Unpruned. Dead. Swaying in storms like clumps of
      August grass. There was much
I wanted to ask: Had my neighbor neglected his taxes? Let rot sap the
      foundation? I held my questions,
fearing I might come to care about the poor man's troubles. I'd not much
      liked the little of him
I'd gotten to know: dirt road built when the county said no. The deer he
      lured into his sights
with blocks of salt. The Dodge he towed across ice and sunk. Left alone, I
      guess, he'd stay

like the barn: passed so often as to make no great impression, a slab of
        Heaney's deep-bog brown
tethering brief seasons to the lives of men. Only at dawn did I understand
        that the barn had become
like a face you regard every day: features so common they register neither
        as fair nor as those
that drive you away — remarkable only when gone. Ask after answers, and
        I'd be liable to find
my neighbor's like hummock that remains: a man who thrives on an
        orchard that yields decay.

Silences

There is a lesson taught when night descends
so hard — no moon, no stars —
you cannot see beyond your heart:
The quality of silence depends
on the nature of the sounds
and the reason for their end.

Across your darkened mind,
the scenes advance, retreat,
like a carousel show of vacations long ago,
and you find your memory clings to only three:

A boy, you march into the marsh,
into the lilt-song, into the flashes of red,
into the silence that flows before you,
that keeps pace with your steps,
so that you never discover
whether blackbirds call and answer
or sing as in a chorus.

The spruce you planted in your youth
lashes shutters, the seaward wall,
then, the wind falls, the tree flags —
spring growth tattered, strewn across the yard —
and the drumming that had tracked your breaths
stops with the force of an alarm.

A woman turns her back
on the question you've asked,
gazes through dimpled glass
to the garden's border,
as if the camellias held the answer.
She lifts fingers to her lips,
lets the roll of her shoulders,
the tilt of her head, convey the message
that pierces deeper than any words can.

On Humboldt Bay

All too soon, she'll give the reins a gentle tug
to turn the rented gelding from the rut
a thousand hooves have cut into the grass-choked dunes.
She never rides the horse she calls her own,
the eight-year-old Arabian roan
the locals claim she paddocks at home
for fear the Marram grass will score the coat.
They can't understand it's hope —
not horse — she keeps penned up. She knows herself
like harbor pilots know the channels' swells:
Without the mount she's paid for by the clock,
she'll spur the flanks and never stop.

December Mornings

Her hand, spread, rides his ribs.
She smiles at his leg's twitch:
hound dreaming after hare.

At first gray light, she slips
from tangled sheets, kindles
last night's fire. The air hints

of smoke — live oak, seasoned.
Last evening's smells surround
her. From the kitchen: garlic

pressed. Near the bed: bees' wax,
mingled sweat. His slacks
and jacket smother shoes,

piled where he dropped them.
The black dress drapes her dressing
table's chair. She wants

to crawl beside him, draw
paired parentheses,
but not enough, to break

his sleep. From the pillow's
creases on his cheek,
she knows she owns

an hour until he'll rise —
time enough to watch
the dawn. Bundled tight,

breath white, she climbs the hill
beyond the orchard where
apples and filberts grow

shagged, last pruned before her birth,
abandoned to meal worms
and blight. Beneath a ruined

branch, she pokes at pulpy
fruit. Gloved hands warm as if
in his, her mind on Dante's

hoarfrost mimes, she does not
catch the sky shade bronze —
the palest kind. On she winds

through heather, moonwort,
the path bordered by bracken,
snowberries, hips of wild

rose. From the crest, land gives
way to mist. The view: crowns
of trees, peak of the farmhouse

roof. No wind, no birds.
The one sound she's heard
as a rasp on wood

she'll learn was an engine's
trying to turn. When
she returns, the clothes

on the floor will have
traveled miles and more.
In the laundry's sink,

she rinses stains,
eliminates all trace
of him except the thought

that wakes with her on bright
December mornings: Love
runs the course of winter's

dawn, flames salmon-pink,
extinguishes, a wick
between finger and thumb.

Notes

The epigraph for this volume, "Everything is water and the world is full of gods," is a quotation from Thales of Miletus, a pre-Socratic Greek astronomer and mathematician whom Aristotle considered the founder of philosophy. This is one of the few fragments of his writing to survive.

"So sweet a lament, that the winds might have stopped to listen" (page 28) is a line from a translation of Ludovico Ariosto's epic *Orlando Furioso*. The first line of the poem is a headline from *The Oregonian* newspaper.

The epigraphs for "Astrophil and Stella" (pages 32 and 33) come from Sir Philip Sidney's *Astrophil and Stella*.

The phrase "bird roads define the sky" (page 51) is a line from the title poem in Bei Dao's *The Rose of Time*.

The inspiration for "The Ohio 1950 Thanksgiving Record Snow" (page 59) and the source of the phrase "for white miles" is Maxine Kumin's "New Hampshire, February 7, 2003."

Sacrum Commercium (page 64) is the title of an allegoric treatise on poverty attributed to the Medieval Franciscan theologian John of Parma.

"I shall be telling this with a sigh" (page 65) is a line from Robert Frost's "The Road Not Taken."